SCIENCE AND INVENTION

MICHAEL REGAN

ignite

Raintree is an imprint of Capstone Global Library Limited, a company incorporated in England and Wales having its registered office at 264 Banbury Road, Oxford, OX2 7DY – Registered company number: 6695582
www.raintree.co.uk
myorders@raintree.co.uk

Text © Capstone Global Library Limited 2017
The moral rights of the proprietor have been asserted.

Edited by Heidi Hogg
Design and production by Nikki Farinella
Original illustrations © Capstone Global Library Limited 2016
Originated by Capstone Global Library Limited
Printed and bound in China

ISBN 978 1 4747 3681 7
20 19 18 17 16
10 9 8 7 6 5 4 3 2 1

British Library Cataloguing in Publication Data
A full catalogue record for this book is available from the British Library.

Acknowledgements
We would like to thank the following for permission to reproduce photographs: Alamy Images: Purestock, 13, Travelscape Images, 21; AP Images: NASA, ESA/Hubble, Hubble Heritage Team, 14; Getty Images: Bettmann, cover, 28, Dennis K. Johnson, 38, Heritage Images/Borthwick Institute, 32, *NY Daily News Archive*/Linda Rosier, 33, VCG/Corbis/Roger Ressmeyer, 30; iStockphoto: hugocorzo, 29, matthewgamble27, 24, Portra, 37; Mary Evans Picture Library, 22; Newscom: EPA/Rolf Haid,10, Ingram Publishing, 25, picture-alliance/Alexander Farnsworth, 9; Photofest: Universal Pictures, 26; Red Line Editorial, 15, 16-17, 35; Science Source, 11; Shutterstock: aeiddam0853578919, 17 (middle right), Anetlanda, 23, Arie v.d. Wolde, 12, borgil, 17 (middle), Dirk Ercken, 36, Dong liu, 40, Everett Historical, 4, Fotos593, 20, Georgios Kollidas, 7, IrinaK, 41, Julie Clopper, 31, Keith Homan, 27, khuruzero, 8, rorem, 34, stock09, 16 (bee icon), 17 (bee icon), Trodler, 39; SuperStock: Fred Hirschmann, 18-19, Interfoto, 5, NHPA, 19 (right); Wellcome Library Rare Books: Conrad Gesner, 6

Design Element: Shutterstock Images: Designer things (bursts, dots, and bubble cloud)

CONTENTS

ANCIENT WEIRDNESS

SCIENTIFIC METHOD GETS SILLY

The history of science and inventions is filled with stunning successes. There have also been many nutty and just plain stupid mistakes made by scientists and inventors throughout the years. Luckily, some of those mistakes have led to impressive discoveries, new ideas and fun inventions. Read on to check out some of the biggest biology blunders, chemical catastrophes, engineering errors and mathematical mistakes.

BACK AWAY FROM THE EDGE!

When did people work out that Earth was round? The 1800s? The 1500s? Earlier? Actually, people in the olden days were more worried about getting eaten by bears than falling off a flat Earth. In the 500s BC, the Greek philosopher and mathematician Pythagoras suggested Earth was round. In the 800s, Christian and Islamic scholars also assumed the world was a sphere. Their only real debate was how far someone had to walk in one direction to get back to his or her starting point. The flat Earth myth, however, started in the 1800s – despite more than 2,300 years of common knowledge that Earth is round.

Even Pythagoras, who lived more than 2,500 years ago, thought Earth was a sphere.

OOPS!

Ancient Greeks and Chinese believed Earth was the centre of the universe. Based on what they could see, Earth stood still, while the sun, stars and planets moved around it.

This geocentric map based on information from the late 1500s shows the planets revolving around Earth.

SO, WHO BELIEVES?

In the 1800s, British inventor Samuel Rowbotham insisted that Earth was flat – despite scientific evidence proving otherwise. He said Earth was a plate centred on the North Pole. Members of the Flat Earth Society, which he founded, still believe and defend the myth to this day. Rowbotham's vision was a platelike planet rimmed by a wall of ice 46 metres (150 feet) tall. Flat-Earthers say the United States's National Aeronautics and Space Administration (NASA) guards the wall of ice. Flat-Earthers believe NASA prevents people from climbing the wall and falling off Earth.

FAST FACT

Before Christopher Columbus tried to sail to Asia from Spain in 1492, he reckoned the trip would be about 5,000 kilometres (3,100 miles). It's actually more like 20,000 kilometres (12,400 miles). The islands of the Bahamas and the whole North American continent – not Asia – happened to be in his path beyond the distance he'd calculated.

SOMETHING FROM NOTHING

Alchemy is the attempt to change one thing into another. The practice was a forerunner to the modern scientific method. A famous example is the ancients' ongoing attempts to turn things into gold. A shame it didn't actually work. Western alchemy started in ancient Egypt. Some alchemists' experiments actually resulted in good stuff, such as formulas for mortar, glass and cosmetics. Other not-so-scientific alchemists believed a substance called the philosopher's stone could help them live forever. These experiments failed, and the practice of alchemy was eventually ridiculed. It did, at least, lay the foundation for modern chemistry. In a little alchemical twist, US nuclear scientists in the 1980s succeeded in getting gold from bismuth, another metal. But it would have cost £1 quadrillion to make one ounce of gold by this method. A pity gold cost only about £430 an ounce at the time.

In the 1500s alchemists tried to create the elixir of life, which was supposed to make a person immortal.

Galileo may have discovered Jupiter's four largest moons, but he seriously underestimated the speed of light.

TOO CLOSE

Galileo Galilei (1564–1642) was a famous Italian scientist. But in the early 1600s, he failed in his attempt to measure the speed of light. He got two assistants to stand on two separate hills with covered lanterns. One assistant uncovered his lantern. As soon as he saw the light, the second assistant uncovered his lantern. Galileo tried to measure the time between the two lantern signals. More than 300 years later, light was measured to travel at about 299,792 kilometres (186,282 miles) per second. The hills were far too close together to measure the speed. Even light from a lantern lit on the moon would take just a little more than a second to reach Earth. Galileo didn't have a very good timing device either – he used his pulse.

FAST FACT

Even the renowned physicist Sir Isaac Newton (1643–1727), who discovered gravity and founded modern physics, was obsessed with alchemy. He wasted years trying to make gold. He also wrote 169 books on the subject in the late 1600s and early 1700s. He didn't publish his books because at the time it was illegal to convert metals into silver or gold.

MEDICAL CURIOSITIES

MAY I HAVE A DIFFERENT DOCTOR, PLEASE?

Galen was the second most-respected physician in the ancient world after Hippocrates. He made many contributions to medicine and the study of the human body during the 100s. But he may have had something in common with vampires! He believed excess blood caused disease. Galen thought bloodletting – cutting into veins and just letting blood flow – would restore the body's balance.

Pacemakers are implanted in people whose hearts beat too slowly, beat too quickly or beat irregularly.

The pacemaker, a medical device that keeps the heart beating smoothly, was a happy accident. American Wilson Greatbatch picked the wrong-sized part out of his toolbox in 1956 while building a different instrument. The device gave Greatbatch an unexpected jolt, and it became the pacemaker. It's now implanted in more than 500,000 people per year.

OOPS!

The Greek doctor Hippocrates, "the Father of Modern Medicine", was born around 460 BC and died in 377 BC. But sometimes he must have been thinking about the great speakers of his time and not biology. He believed veins carried hot air, not blood.

BAD MEDICINE

Qin Shihuangdi, the first emperor of China, wanted to live forever. He should have known this never ends well. His doctors and alchemists searched the world to find a magic formula. They made pills loaded with mercury, which the emperor took daily. He died in 210 BC of mercury poisoning, aged 49.

After death, Qin Shihuangdi was buried with more than 6,000 terracotta soldiers he believed would guard him in the afterlife.

DID YOU KNOW?

Ever wonder how long it would take a vampire to drain just enough blood from your body and not kill you? Physics students at the University of Leicester, share your creepy curiosity. In 2015 they reckoned it would take 6.4 minutes, or less if the vampire was sucking.

CHECK YOUR WORK

HOW HIGH IS THE SEA?

German and Swiss builders began constructing a bridge in 2003 that spanned the river Rhine. The bridge was supposed to connect the German and Swiss halves of the town of Laufenburg. Fine. Except Germans measure sea level based on the North Sea, and the Swiss measure sea level based on the Mediterranean Sea. They're not the same. The different measurements resulted in the German side being 53 centimetres (21 inches) higher than the Swiss side. As construction on the bridge progressed, it became obvious the two sides would not match. The German side was lowered to match the height of the Swiss side.

German engineers lowered their part of the bridge on the right to match the Swiss side on the left.

The successful launch of Sputnik sparked the Space Race between the Soviet Union and the United States.

The Soviet Union successfully launched Sputnik, the first satellite, into orbit in October 1957. The United States was desperate to keep up. It tried to launch its own satellite in December 1957 with the Vanguard TV3 rocket. The rocket exploded shortly after launch, and many newspapers labelled the attempt as "Kaputnik".

OOPS!

MEASURE TWICE, CUT ONCE

Suck in your stomach and watch your toes! Newspapers reported in 2016 that the French national railway had purchased 2,000 new railway carriages. Unfortunately, they were too wide for 1,300 of the railway's older station platforms. Since rail carriages can't go on a diet, the station platforms had to be shaved to accommodate the new trains.

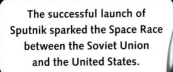

FAST FACT

Air Canada's first aircraft to use the metric system took a short flight in 1983. The ground crew mistakenly converted the plane's volume of fuel to pounds rather than kilograms. The plane ended up carrying only half the fuel they thought. After taking off from Montréal, Québec, it made a successful emergency landing at the Gimli airfield in Manitoba. The plane became known as the Gimli Glider.

NOT ON THE SAME PAGE

A little communication, please? The Mars Climate Orbiter was supposed to collect data on Mars weather. NASA collaborated with the US company Lockheed Martin to build it. Lockheed Martin engineers used feet and pounds to measure force. Unfortunately, the metric system, which measures force in metres and newtons, is standard for space missions. NASA engineers failed to check that measurements were converted to the metric system before liftoff. The result? The £96 million Mars Climate Orbiter, launched in 1999, entered too far into the Martian atmosphere and burned up. The rest of the mission was scrapped.

Boeing built the 707 from 1958 to 1979.

FAST FACT

Copying someone else's work is not only unfair – it can totally flop. In the 1970s China bought a US Boeing 707 with the goal of copying it and building its own airliners. But engineers miscalculated the plane's centre of gravity . . . and it couldn't fly.

GETTING IT RIGHT

After a severe scolding from NASA bigwigs, engineers got the next one right. NASA launched the wildly successful Mars Exploration Rovers *Spirit* and *Opportunity* in 2003. As of early 2016, almost 12 years after it landed on Mars, *Opportunity* is still exploring the red planet. It's a testament to what can happen when you pay attention to detail.

Mars Exploration Rover *Opportunity* is still sending data back to Earth.

BABY NEEDS NEW GLASSES

NASA launched the Hubble Space Telescope into low Earth orbit in 1990 at a cost of £1.1 billion. A microscopic mistake would result in one of the most expensive scientific blunders of all time. As soon as the telescope reached orbit, astronomers pointed it into space to look at stuff. They immediately noticed a huge problem. The images Hubble sent back were so fuzzy that the telescope was unusable. After a thorough investigation, scientists realized the main mirror of the telescope had been ground too thin at the edges during manufacture. The mistake was a depth of only 2.2 micrometres, about 1/50th the thickness of a human hair. Investigators eventually discovered what caused the 2.2-micrometre mistake. Technicians had assembled a rod in the grinding device incorrectly, and they slapped on some 15 pence washers to make it fit. Rather than give up on what had become a very expensive piece of space junk, NASA decided to save it. Over the course of five spacewalks, they added five pairs of corrective mirrors and two new cameras to adjust Hubble's vision. The remedy worked.

After fixing the mirrors, the Hubble Space Telescope sent back breathtaking pictures of the universe, including this one, called the Pillars of Creation.

American Don McPherson specialized in making lab glasses for doctors to use when doing laser surgery. In 2005 one of his friends tried them on and discovered he could see orange traffic cones nearby. The friend was colourblind. McPherson's glasses help about 80 per cent of the colourblind people who have tried them.

The image on the left is how a person without colourblindness perceives colour. The image on the right is how a person with red-green colourblindness sees colour.

MESSING WITH PLANTS AND ANIMALS

FRANKENBEES

European honeybees thrive in the temperate climate of North America, but they don't do so well in tropical South America. Warwick Kerr, a Brazilian scientist, decided to breed feisty, sturdy honeybees from Africa with gentle European honeybees. He thought the new hybrids might just solve Brazil's bee problem. Kerr imported bees from Africa in the late 1950s and put them under quarantine so they wouldn't get away. Unfortunately, a local beekeeper wandered by and mistakenly removed a small piece of equipment called a queen excluder. This allowed 26 queen bees to make a mad dash for freedom.

African bees felt quite at home in South America. They quickly moved north, mating with European honeybees along the way. The hybridized bees – called Africanized honeybees – started to take over European honeybee colonies. As of 2012 Africanized honeybees were in the US states of Texas, California, New Mexico, Arizona, Oklahoma, Louisiana, Arkansas, Alabama and Florida.

THE DISTANCE BEES WILL FOLLOW VICTIMS WHO DISTURB THE HIVE

45 METRES

| 0 metres | 50 | 100 | 150 | 200 |

A French scientist living in Massachusetts, USA, imported some gypsy moth caterpillars in 1869. He wanted to crossbreed them with American silk-moth caterpillars to make a stronger thread. But some of the gypsy moth caterpillars escaped. The breed now eats all the leaves on millions of hectares of trees in the region of New England.

OOPS!

O, WHAT'S E PROBLEM?

It turns out that canized bees are exactly friendly. ct, their nickname the story – bees. When rbed, killer bees k in greater numbers over larger distances than ary honeybees. These insects cause about man deaths per year.

It can be hard to tell the difference between European honeybees (left) and Africanized honeybees (right).

fricanized honeybees will follow their victims more than eight times farther than European honeybees.

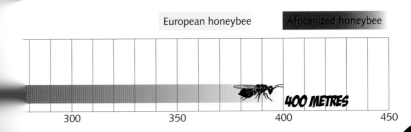

European honeybee   Africanized honeybee

400 METRES

300   350   400   450

HEY! I MAY BE OLD, BUT I'M NOT DEAD YET

Bristlecone pines can live thousands of years. Donald Currey was a 29-year-old geographer. He wanted to take a core sample from a bristlecone pine in Nevada, USA, in 1964 to learn the tree's age. But his corer got stuck in the tree. Helpful park rangers chopped down the tree and retrieved the corer. Later, Currey counted the rings. He discovered they'd killed the oldest tree ever recorded – it was almost 5,000 years old! At least the tree's death prompted the creation of the Great Basin National Park to protect other bristlecone pines.

FAST FACT

All is not lost for old bristlecones. An even older tree was discovered in 2016 in the White Mountains of California, USA. It is thought to be older than 5,000 years.

THE CLAM

If you were to dig up a dozen quahogs – a type of clam – from the seabed, they might all be older than your granddad. A team of scientists from Bangor University in Wales took some quahogs from the Icelandic sea in 2006. The scientists froze them to take home and study. When they later counted the quahogs' growth rings, they found that one of them was 507 years old. It was the oldest living animal ever discovered! The scientists were soundly criticized for killing it. "We had no idea it was that old before it was too late," one of the team members said.

This bristlecone pine at the Great Basin National Park looks just like an average size tree, but it is thousands of years old.

This quahog found near Scotland can also live more than 500 years.

DID YOU KNOW?

The Bangor scientists named their quahog Ming. The name comes from the Chinese dynasty in power when the quahog was born . . . in 1499. The Ming dynasty was long-lived too, lasting almost 300 years.

The Giant Tortoise of the Galapagos Islands wasn't recorded in science books for 300 years after its discovery. The tortoises were so tasty that sailors ate them on their voyages home before the animals could be catalogued.

The Giant Tortoise is now a protected animal in the Galapagos Islands.

THIS TOAD IS NO PRINCE

Australian farmers in the 1930s had a big problem with beetles devouring their sugarcane fields. So they asked for help from the Queensland Department of Agriculture. Bug expert Reginald Mungomery had an idea. He would import cane toads from Hawaii to eat the beetles. But Mungomery didn't test first to see if cane toads would even eat native Australian beetles. After a couple of thousand toads were released in Queensland, people saw the amphibians quickly bypass the cane fields' yukky-tasting bugs. Instead, the toads quickly multiplied and became pests themselves. Originally 102 toads were set loose in 1935. The cane toad's numbers had grown to more than 2 billion by 2011. They had invaded more than 1 million square kilometres (386,000 square miles) of Australia by 2016. That's an area roughly the size of Egypt.

Oh, did you know that cane toads are also poisonous? They may look fat and juicy (the biggest cane toad ever found was the size of a Chihuahua dog), but their skin oozes toxic venom. Dead kangaroos, dogs and other animals that have tried to eat cane toads now litter the countryside. Experts have tried trapping, messing around with the toad's DNA and poisoning, but nothing controls them. It seems Australia is stuck with the cane toad for a long time to come.

DID YOU KNOW?

Cane toad races are popular tourist attractions in Australia. After capturing some of the hated amphibians, race officials put numbers on the toads. The toads are then placed in the centre of a large circle. The first toad to reach the circle's edge wins. This family-friendly event may be the only time cane toads are loudly cheered on.

Cane toad racing in Queensland, Australia

BAD MISTAKES TURN GOOD!

DIRTY DISCOVERY

Leaving dirty dishes in the sink isn't always a bad thing. Scottish scientist Alexander Fleming went on holiday and left some petri dishes in his lab in 1928. They contained failed experiments for a wonder drug he'd been trying to create. After returning, he cleaned out his lab and found one petri dish was particularly interesting. It was mouldy and gross, but he noticed there were no bacteria in the dish – the mould had killed them. Fleming had discovered the antibiotic penicillin, one of the greatest advances in medicine.

Alexander Fleming with his microscope

DID YOU KNOW?

Nitrous oxide (also called laughing gas) was used as party entertainment for rich people in the mid-1800s. It stopped being a laughing matter when it was discovered to be a good tranquilliser around 1863. Laughing gas is still used by dentists and doctors to relax their patients.

I DARE YOU TO DRINK THIS!

Danish researchers Eric Jacobsen and Jens Hald were experimenting with a substance that might fight stomach bugs in 1947. They took some of the stuff themselves, which was a dangerous but not unusual thing scientists did at the time. They later went to a party where they drank alcohol and proceeded to get very sick. Their discovery led to the drug Antabuse, which is now used to discourage drinking in alcoholics.

ROTTEN FOOD TO THE RESCUE?

An anxious farmer visited American biochemist Karl Paul Link in 1933. Some of the farmer's cows had started bleeding to death. Research by Link showed the cows' rotten hay had an ingredient called an anticoagulant. Anticoagulants make it hard for blood to clot. The cows just needed fresh food. But the substance found in the bad hay was made into a drug called warfarin. This blood thinner is now given to people to help prevent heart attacks and strokes.

Cut yourself? Just rub this mouldy bread on it!

FAST FACT

Same use, different name. Mouldy bread, probably containing penicillin, has been used since ancient Egyptian times to disinfect cuts.

FIREWORKS FROM THE KITCHEN

The Chinese had pretty good firecrackers as early as 200 BC. They would throw pieces of bamboo on a fire, and the air pockets in the sticks would explode. About 1,000 years later, the Chinese made a more powerful firework. For some reason, someone mixed together saltpetre (commonly used to season food at the time), charcoal, sulphur and some other substances. The accidental creation was an early form of gunpowder. The mixture was stuffed in a bamboo tube, thrown on a fire, and KABOOM!

China produces and exports more fireworks than any other country in the world. The city of San Diego, California, USA, purchased 7,000 of them in 2012 for its Big Bay Boom. The show was supposed to last about 17 minutes, but the fireworks were accidentally lit all at once.

OOPS!

The Big Bay Boom fireworks display went much more smoothly in 2015.

I'M MELTING!

If a chocolate bar started melting in your pocket, you might not think the same thing that Percy Spencer did: "It must be microwaves!" The American scientist was using microwaves as a way to power radar equipment in 1945. Then the chocolate bar in his pocket melted. Intrigued, Spencer experimented with corn kernels and a few other foods. The microwave oven was born. Future engineers made sure the microwaves were contained in a machine so they wouldn't cook the cook!

The first microwaves had fewer buttons than the microwaves of today.

I'LL SHOW YOU CRISPY!

A customer at a café near Saratoga Springs, New York, USA, ordered a plate of fried potatoes in 1853. He kept sending the plate back to the kitchen because the potatoes weren't crispy enough. The annoyed chef decided to get revenge. He cut them into thin slices, severely overcooked them and threw on a lot of salt. Surprisingly, the customer loved them and ordered more. The potato crisp was born.

FAST FACT

Potato crisps got stale and soggy easily because they were originally stored in barrels or tins. Solution: an airtight bag! This food saver was invented by US businesswoman Laura Scudder in 1926.

In the 1982 movie *E.T. the Extra-Terrestrial*, the director wanted to use M&M sweets to lure the space creature. The company declined permission, not wanting M&M's to be associated with aliens. The director substituted Reese's Pieces, a popular US sweet. Reeses overtook M&M's in total sales when the movie became a hit.

OOPS!

In the movie, the main character, Elliott, used Reese's Pieces to bring E.T. back to his house.

Ruth Wakefield's recipe led to the creation of Nestlé's chocolate chips.

CHUNKY SUBSTITUTE

One day in 1930 Ruth Wakefield ran out of cooking chocolate for her tasty chocolate cookies. Wakefield was the owner of the Toll House Inn, in the state of Massachusetts, USA. She substituted pieces of a Nestlé's semisweet chocolate bar, thinking they'd melt. Except they didn't melt and left little chunks of chocolate in the cookies. Embarrassed but not willing to let food go to waste, Wakefield served the cookies anyway. Her customers raved about them, and sweet-toothed souls everywhere began their love affair with the chocolate chip cookie.

DID YOU KNOW?

The Nestlé company gave Ruth Wakefield, the chocolate-chip-cookie inventor, a lifetime supply of chocolate bars. However, she did not receive any money in exchange for allowing her recipe to be printed on every Nestlé semisweet chocolate product.

CONGRATULATIONS, IT'S A TOY!

NOT A SPRINGING SUCCESS

At the beginning of World War II (1939–1945), US Navy engineer Richard James began tinkering. He wanted to develop springs to stabilize sensitive instruments on ships that sailed through rough seas. He accidentally knocked some parts off a shelf and watched in wonder. A spring seemed to "walk" across a desk, down several levels of books and onto the floor. He reportedly spent the rest of the day playing with the spring. It later dawned on him he'd just invented an awesome toy. That night he took it home, and his wife came up with a name – the Slinky.

Children in the 1940s were fascinated by the Slinky.

YOU'VE GOT TO SEE IT IN ACTION!

James spent a year perfecting the toy and then tried to sell it to toy shops without much success. He kept at it until a department store in Philadelphia, Pennsylvania, USA, agreed to sell the Slinky. It went on sale in November 1945, but no one bought it. James was certain the toy would be a hit if people could only see it in action. So he went to the shop, sat down with children and demonstrated how the toy worked. Within 90 minutes he had sold all 400 of the toys. Altogether, 20,000 Slinkys sold before Christmas that year.

FAST FACT

Kids keep falling in love with the Slinky, even 70 years after the toy was first introduced. More than 350 million have been sold worldwide as of 2015.

Slinkies today come in a rainbow of colours.

DID YOU KNOW?

In order to revive interest in the Slinky in 1962, an advertising jingle was created. For more than 20 years, slightly different versions of the jingle were used in television commercials on American TV. It became the longest-running jingle in the history of US television advertising.

TYRE FAILURE, TOY SUCCESS

Engineer James Wright was working at a lab in Connecticut, USA, during World War II. He was attempting to create a rubber substitute for aeroplane tyres and army boots. Instead, he created a gooey, bouncy mess that stretched too much and snapped in two when yanked quickly. Wright and his bosses dismissed the substance as a failure. But they sent it to other scientists to see if they could come up with a use for it. Peter Hodgson, a marketing expert, saw the goo's potential as a toy. He bought the rights to it for £113 in 1950 and packaged it in a plastic egg-shaped container. By the time Hodgson died in 1976, he was worth £108 million from sales of Silly Putty. Bad luck for Wright!

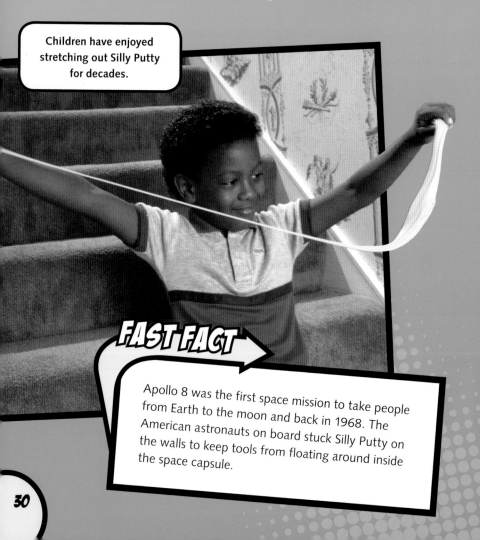

Children have enjoyed stretching out Silly Putty for decades.

FAST FACT

Apollo 8 was the first space mission to take people from Earth to the moon and back in 1968. The American astronauts on board stuck Silly Putty on the walls to keep tools from floating around inside the space capsule.

DID YOU KNOW?

Central American Indians mastered making rubber long before it was used for tyres. The Maya, Olmec and Aztec people made statues, glue and balls for games from rubber. Spanish explorers in the 1500s noted the Aztec wore rubber-soled shoes.

CLEAN YOUR ROOM!

Play-Doh was first sold in the 1930s by Americans Joseph McVicker and Bill Rhodenbaugh. It wasn't a toy, though. It was a wallpaper cleaner, useful when sooty coal was still used to heat homes. After World War II, natural gas replaced coal as a heat source. That meant no more soot and no more need for the cleaning product. McVicker's sister-in-law Kay Zufall, a teacher, used the stuff as modelling clay in her class in the early 1950s. She convinced McVicker to rename the cleaning product Play-Doh, and he started selling it in 1956. Play-Doh made McVicker a lot of money. But in 1965, McVicker decided to sell Play-Doh to General Mills for £2.3 million. Rhodenbaugh thought the deal was a bad idea – because it was. From 2009 to 2014, sales of Play-Doh topped £606 million.

Play-Doh is a staple in most preschool classrooms.

THAT BYTES

THE END OF THE WORLD?

In the 1990s people feared all the computers in the world would fail on 1 January 2000. The Millennium Bug (year 2000 bug) was the result of how computers were programmed in the 1960s. Those old-fashioned computers had very limited memory, so programmers abbreviated dates down to two numbers. For example, 1971 would have been 71. People feared that computers would not be able to tell the difference between 2000 and 1900. They thought computer programmes would freeze, resulting in planes falling out of the sky, massive power failures and banks shutting down.

Computer programmers worked feverishly to fix the bug, spending an estimated £230 billion worldwide. In the days and months leading up to 1 January 2000, people began hoarding food, fuel, water, money and other necessities. They were preparing for when the lights went off and mayhem broke loose. The British government announced its armed forces would be ready to provide help to local police.

Computers from the 1960s were much larger than they are now.

Close to 2 million people packed into Times Square, New York, USA, to celebrate the year 2000.

MEH

The big day came, and . . . nothing. No major problems were reported anywhere. Even countries where little had been done to combat the problem, such as Italy, Russia and South Korea, were fine. Either the bug was fixed in time, or it wasn't as big a problem as many had thought. Instead, people had a great Millennium party – and they had lots of leftover tinned food.

Counting from 1970, all of the 2,147,483,647 spaces needed for current computers to record dates down to the second will be used up on 19 January 2038. Will there be more panic buying of tinned beans next time?

OOPS!

COMPUTER BLIP, POWER OUT

A small bit of computer code wreaked major havoc on 14 August 2003. It toppled the power network in parts of the United States and Canada like dominos. It all started in the state of Ohio, USA, where a software bug turned off an alarm system. The alarm would have warned operators that something was wrong. Within hours, electric power lines and power plants were cut off because of a huge power surge, crossing country borders. It was the biggest power crisis in American history.

In all, 256 power plants shut down between Toronto in Ontario, Canada, and Ohio. In New York City, thousands of passengers had to be evacuated from lifts and subway tunnels. The governor estimated 600 trains were stranded. Although the lights did not go out everywhere, an estimated 50 million people were affected in Canada and the United States.

During the August 2003 outage, 600 trains in New York City were at a standstill.

Outages occurred in all of these states and provinces (red) during the Northeast blackout of 2003.

N
W E
S

FAST FACT

The Soviet Union stole gas pipeline software in the 1980s. The United States knew of the plot beforehand and created a software bug just for the Soviets. The bug reset valve settings and pump speeds to extremely high levels. The resulting blast was seen from space by satellites.

WHAT WERE THEY THINKING?

THE BABY SPEAKS CHIMP

Just because you can imagine a crazy experiment doesn't mean you should do it. American psychologist Winthrop Kellogg had been fascinated by stories of wild children raised in nature with no human contact. He decided in 1931 to do an experiment to see how the environment affects how children grow up. He brought a baby chimpanzee into his home and raised it exactly the same as his own baby boy. Kellogg stopped the experiment nine months later. The chimp was not learning human language . . . and his son began barking like a chimp.

Chimpanzees aren't always cute and cuddly.

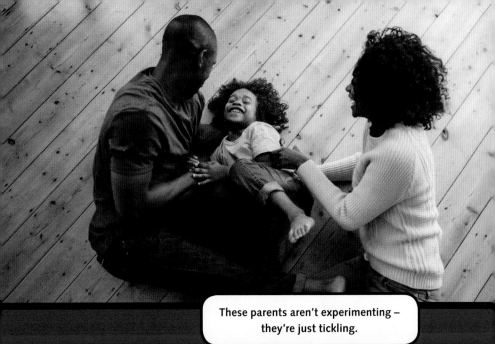

These parents aren't experimenting – they're just tickling.

THAT'S NOT FUNNY!

The 1930s seemed to be a popular time for experimenting on your own children. US psychologist Clarence Leuba set out to see why people learn to laugh. He wondered if it is because they are tickled or because it's in our nature as humans. Once a day he put on a mask, so his son could not see his facial expressions. He then tickled his son. He also did the same experiment with his daughter. He learned two important things: laughing comes naturally, and tickling works best along the ribs and under the arms. What was never reported was if, for the rest of their lives, his children laughed every time they saw someone in a mask.

FAST FACT

These experiments would not take place today. Scientific communities around the world generally follow a strict code of ethics. Scientists must follow rules about getting permission from everyone they experiment on. They also have to prove the experiment will not do more harm than good before they can begin.

ACCIDENTAL TEEN BOMBER?

In April 2013, 16-year-old American high school student Kiera Wilmot tested out the chemistry project she'd brought to school. What could possibly go wrong? While Kiera expected some smoke, she hadn't anticipated the reaction of her school in Florida. School officials thought she was trying to make a bomb and called the police. Kiera was arrested and faced expulsion from school. The charges were eventually dropped, and Kiera returned to school for her final year. Homer Hickam, a former lead astronaut trainer for NASA, believed Kiera was a budding scientist, not a bomber. He paid for her to attend the five-day United States Advanced Space Academy.

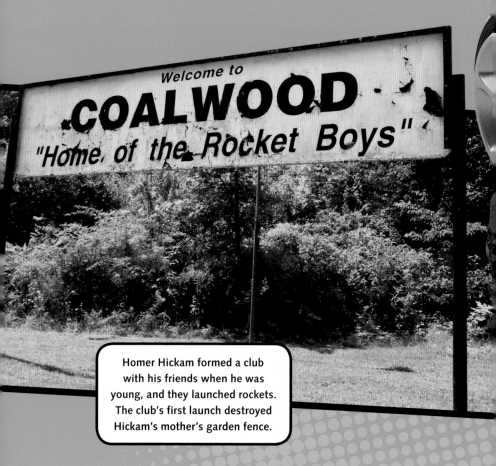

Homer Hickam formed a club with his friends when he was young, and they launched rockets. The club's first launch destroyed Hickam's mother's garden fence.

FAST FACT

Kiera Wilmot graduated from high school in June 2014. She was accepted at Florida Polytechnic University and is studying mechanical and robotic engineering.

In most cases, a faulty battery is to blame for hoverboards catching fire.

DID YOU KNOW?

D'you like blowing things up? Well we've got a job for you! Underwriters Laboratories is a company that tests the safety of new products. It created a test to find out which hoverboards might accidentally explode. The test results will help build safer boards in the future.

NEXT PROJECT: FIRE EXTINGUISHER

It is probably best not to try this science project at home. A 14-year-old British student was just trying to duplicate the Bunsen burner he had made in a chemistry class one day in 2015. Using an empty aluminium can and hairspray, his science experiment caught fire and ended up burning down a block of flats. Luckily no one was killed, but the blunder left more than 100 people homeless and caused £3 million in damages.

ANIMALS STRIKE BACK

WHERE'S THE SECURITY GUARD?

Engineers working on the Large Hadron Collider never thought they'd be sabotaged by a weasel. But the £5.4 billion, 27-kilometre (17-mile) long superconducting science machine in Switzerland suddenly stopped working in early 2016. It seemed a weasel had gnawed through a power cable. Unfortunately, the little chap didn't live to tell the tale. Raccoons attacked a similar machine in the United States years earlier. The raccoons got away, and no human operators were injured in the stealth attack.

The Large Hadron Collider is located at CERN, the European Organization for Nuclear Research, in Switzerland.

Three mice infected with the plague escaped from a research lab in the United States in 2005. The lab urged people not to worry, but we'll see how relaxed that spokesperson is when the mice come to his house! Local hospitals later reported no evidence of human infection.

WONDERFUL NUTTY FLAVOUR

A squirrel's teeth can cause a lot of damage.

Level 3 Communications is a worldwide communications provider that uses underground fibre-optic cables. The second-biggest cause of service interruptions to its systems is squirrels that chew on cables. They accounted for 17 percent of the company's fibre-optic damage in 2011.

DID YOU KNOW?

At the Sea Star Aquarium in Coburg, Germany, Otto the octopus found the light shining in his tank at night annoying. So he shot a stream of water at it, shortcircuiting all the electricity to the aquarium.

FUN FACTS

*T*he philosopher's stone was a legendary powder, not an actual rock.

*T*hirteen-year-old British schoolboy Jamie Edwards became the youngest person in the world to build a nuclear reactor in 2014. He built it in his school lab and even had his teacher's permission!

*R*esearchers working at a laboratory in the United States in the 2010s were trying to make microscopic magnetic wires (nanowires). Instead, they accidentally created something called nanorods. Nanorods collect the water in the air around them. They wring themselves out like sponges when the humidity reaches 50 to 80 per cent. Researchers hope to use the "mistake" to get water from desert air and remove sweat from clothing.

*C*hinese scientist Rongxiang Xu thinks he's brilliant. Really brilliant. He sued Sweden's Karolinska Institute, which awards the Nobel Prize for Physiology or Medicine, in 2012. Apparently Xu thought his contributions to medicine that year meant he deserved the prize.

*G*enesis was a US space probe that collected some solar wind for scientists to study. It was supposed to return to Earth in 2004. But the parachute failed to open on its trip back. The craft slammed into Earth's surface at close to 322 kilometres (200 miles) per hour. The spacecraft had sensors that should have deployed the parachute and slowed the capsule to a safe speed for landing. Investigators discovered the sensors had been built upside down.

*I*f you were bald in England in the 1600s, medical journals had a cure for you. Apparently rubbing some chicken dung on the top of your head was supposed to do the trick. It stinks that it didn't actually work.

*T*he Big Bang Theory got its name from a physicist who actually opposed this idea about how the universe began. Fred Hoyle thought that giving Georges Lemaître's theory a ridiculous name would help discredit it. Instead, Hoyle's beliefs about an unchanging universe were abandoned.

*M*anufactured chocolate chips weren't created until after American cafe owner Ruth Wakefield whipped up her now-famous recipe for chocolate chip cookies. After securing the recipe, Nestlé invented the teardrop-shaped chocolate chip in 1939.

GLOSSARY

alchemy early chemistry that did not use the scientific method

debate discussion between two sides with different ways of thinking on a subject; each side tries to convince people that it is right

discredit harm the good reputation of someone or something

DNA molecule of which genes are made

extraterrestrial creature from outer space

formula combination of chemicals used to change something

hoverboard self-balancing scooter

hybridize mix of two species

mercury poisonous chemical element given off by burning certain fossil fuels

microscopic too small to be seen without a microscope

newton unit of force

petri dish shallow, circular transparent dish used for growing organisms

philosopher's stone mythical substance supposed to change any metal into gold or silver

plague disease that spreads quickly and kills most people who catch it

quarantine act of keeping something separate from a larger group

saltpetre another name for potassium nitrate

scholar person who has done advanced study in a special field

tranquillizer drug used to reduce tension or anxiety

washer small flat ring made of metal, rubber or plastic

FIND OUT MORE

BOOKS

Mistakes That Worked: 40 Familiar Inventions and How They Came to Be, Charlotte Foltz Jones (Doubleday, 2013).

Rebel Science, Dan Green (Sterling, 2016).

Science: A Children's Encyclopedia, Chris Woodford and Steve Parker (Dorling Kindersley, 2014).

Women in Science: 50 Fearless Pioneers Who Changed the World, Rachel Ignotofsky (Ten Speed Press, 2016).

WEBSITES

Scientists and Discoveries
http://www.bbc.co.uk/education/topics/zw44jxs/resources/1
Watch video clips about scientists and inventors from the past and today.

Science Sparks
http://www.science-sparks.com/
Launch your own scientific investigation with experiment ideas from this website.

FURTHER RESEARCH

Many scientists and inventors earn money for their discoveries and creations by applying for patents or trademarks. What can you learn about how patents and trademarks work in the UK? Try searching online or asking a teacher for help.

Imagine you are a scientist who has just discovered a new life-saving drug. Should you apply for a patent or let all drug companies sell the new drug? Look up how much it costs to develop a new drug. Does that change your answer?

PLACES TO VISIT

Science Museum
Exhibition Road
London SW7 2DD
Tel: +44 (0)207 7942 4000
www.sciencemuseum.org.uk
Four floors of fascinating interactive galleries, simulators and technology make this museum a "must see" for anyone interested in scientific discovery and inventions.

The Ironbridge Gorge Museums
Coach Road
Coalbrookdale
Telford
Shropshire
TF8 7DQ
Tel: +44 (0)1952 433424
www.ironbridge.org.uk
Find out about some of the pioneers of industry and the machines they invented that helped to kick-start the Industrial Revolution.

INDEX